D1534985

How To Start A Candle Business

Matthew Heintschel

CONTENTS

HOW TO START A CANDLE BUSINESS

1. BREAKING POINT

Sitting by the dumpster with the 300 candles I had made just a month and a half earlier. As tears run down my cheek, I sit there and ask myself " what was I thinking?" Why did I believe I could do this? Go to any store, look at the competition. I thought to myself. "How could this have ever worked?" It seemed like all my dreams have collapsed right in front of me, making the summer an absolute rollercoaster ride. I went from the highs off the idea that I would be able to avoid the rat race that all my other peers where about to dive head first into. To the lows of not getting to do what I loved, but also losing every penny I had investing into this candle business.

At this time I was living in an apartment with three other friends and unfortunately if I couldn't sell all these candles I had just made, they were about to take up every square foot of livable space in my room. Besides all the room they were taking up, every time I looked at them it was like taking a right hook straight to the face. "I am a failure" I told myself as I launched the first box of candles into the dumpster. The sound of all the glass hitting the empty metal walls of the dumpster practically blew out my ear drum as all my hard work shattered right before my eyes.

My ears ringing as if a grenade had just gone off. Despite all the negative feelings I had just felt, at that moment I had one last jolt of hope. I thought one more time, maybe there is one more thing I could try, one more attempt and this all would be easier to accept. I sat down for a minute with the 288 candles I had left and just had a moment to slow down and think. When I first started that was probably my biggest issue, I never took a second to just think. While I wonder thinking back what all the cars driving past must have thought when they saw me sitting with my back against the dumpster and a ton of candles next to me, that was probably the most important minute that complete changed the trajectory of the candle business.

Without skipping a beat I picked up all my candles and ran inside. I felt this instant lightness like I had this fresh new start on everything. As soon as I got back inside I just started looking at images of candles and looking at the seemingly endless size, shape, brands, scents. There has got to be a way, it seems like there are thousands of candles businesses that have found their way. I decided that I am back in the candle business.

NEVER FORGET THIS CONCEPT
If you take one concept from this book, it will be to push through when it seems like you are at your

breaking point. I wish there was an easier way to put this, but you will hit a point where you question if you made the right decisions, I believe that it is those who preserve and continue when it seems all the odds are against them will be the ones to succeed in this business. Now let me be clear, this book will share with you all of my secrets on how to build a successful candle business, but you have to ask yourself "will I be able to smash that fear and keep going when things get tough?"

YOU ARE THE DRIVER AND EDUCATION IS THE KEY

Now luckily for you, you are already one step ahead of me. It is my guess you are reading this book because you probably have a burning in your soul to make this business work. I will be honest, I didn't take that step in getting educated before starting my business. I had more of a run and gun approach which led me to make many mistakes that could have been avoided. That would have saved me a ton money and time! Have you asked yourself why you want to start a candle business? In the next chapter I will explain why I believe the candle business makes the perfect start up, but if I have to think about the "why" it would have been that I wanted to do something I liked on my own terms! I figured that if it someday made a ton of money that would be a great bonus, but I wanted nothing more than to be able to do something I loved without having to report to a boss who couldn't care less about me. I had heard horror stories of people going out into the "corporate world" and doing work they hated their entire life, living for the weekends and dreading Monday. How could anyone fall into this trap? Trading five days you hate for 2 days of fun, week after week? This five for two trade for me didn't make sense. Would you trade $5 for $2 dollars? Probably not, and this was my drive to figure out a business I could do on my terms and waking up excited for whatever I had planned that day.

LEARN THE FUNDIMENTALS OF GROWING AN EXPLOSIVE CANDLE BUSINESS

How will this book help you achieve whatever your goals are with your candle business? Well to begin, I have seen countless "how to" candle books that provided nothing but information and how to make 1000 different types of candles, but no mentoring, no suggestions on to sell the products you make, no tips with building a website, and just focusing just on making a candle is the quickest way to end up sitting by a dumpster like I was. You see, you could have the best candle in the world, but without a way to sell it, you will be the only person to ever have that candle. It is my mission to give you all the tips I have learned throughout growing my candle business, so we can get your business up and growing in no time!

THE PRINCIPALS OF SUCCESS

In this book we are going to cover:
- Where to begin
- What to make so customers can't resist
- How to catch the eye of the customer
- Where to sell your candles for explosive sales

- How to create a website that sells
- Create powerful marketing
- And how to take action today

Do you notice one bullet point of the seven is what to make? The truth is what to make is such a small part of what leads to a profitable, growing candle business. You have to be well rounded in all those bullet points, which is why I am going to share with you all the secrets I learned.

WHO AM I & $200,000 A MONTH?!

So at this point you are probably asking who am I and have I actually ever created a profitable candle business? My name is Matthew Heintschel and I have done just that. The best part? It wasn't something that took 20 years to get to the point of doing very well, in fact it only took a couple months. My low of the dumpster moment was the summer of 2017, I had no sales and little hope for my candle business. So when did I sell my first candle? September of 2017, just two months after I had almost given up completely. That first sale was the best feeling I have ever had. It was a proof of concept for me and gave me a boost of confidence that helped propel my business into a hyper fast growing machine.

With this new boost of hope I started asking all my friends I could find to help me to start making candles. We kept finding better ways to do things to increase how many we could make in a given time. In the next few months I had grown the candle business from $0 in sales to selling $200,000 a month! Yes, you read that correctly a month!

The figure below shows my seller dashboard,

which recorded all my sales real time. On the left you can see my first sale, just $32.77 and a few months later I had hit $91,590 in just the first 18 days of the month!

Now, I will let you know at this point I didn't have the free time I wanted, but it didn't matter. I was doing what I loved every day! I got to hang out with friends and make candles! This is the life I had always dreamed of! This became life changing and opened my eyes to the fact you really can do whatever you want in life, and that you don't have to "settle" for a life you don't enjoy.

Chapter Takeaways:

- If you take the time to learn about the candle business first you will save time and money.
- Learning to make the candle is one of the least important parts of the business.
- Don't listen to the "how to" books that don't actually explain the business side of candles
- You will hit your "turning point", you need to push past that to succeed.
- Growth can happen quickly! It does not take years.

2. THE PERFECT START-UP

SILICON VALLEY, WE DON'T NEED YOU:
You hear about all these "tech startups" raising millions of dollars before they can start. For me I didn't have the time or connections to probably do something like that. I had to think of a business of a business I could start with my total budget of about $600. A really long way from millions, so I figured there was no way I would think about an expensive new start up idea. As much as I wanted to create the next big social media site or the next big computer company, I knew it was just not possible at the time. So I started researching businesses I could start with little to no money. I started seeing things like start a

car wash or photography. The worst I came across was starting a junk removal service and I knew that was not something I could picture myself doing.

After a long brainstorming session, I thought that there was no magic idea that I was going to be able to try, until I had my light bulb moment. "That's it! A candle business!" I immediately started convincing myself why it was the perfect idea. I thought, "everyone has a candle in their home!" Besides the fact that I do believe probably almost everyone has had a candle or has a candle in their home showed me that there in fact was a huge demand! Even if you don't own a candle, how many Christmas gatherings have you been too where at least someone gets a candle? I know everyone at mine always gets one!

At the time I knew some friends that made candles for fun in their free time. I figured that would be a very cheap start up because they had no fancy tools or anything to make them. I also figured the supplies couldn't have cost that much. As I started looking into the candle business it appeared this was a business with huge opportunity and could be fun!

Since you have picked up this book and chose to read it also, you probably have already experienced that light bulb moment! Congratulations! I think you are on to a really great idea so far. After considering so many other business ideas, candles really seemed like the best one!

CONTROL IS IN YOUR HANDS

When you make the product you control all the aspects. This might sound scary, but let me explain why this is so great just starting off. Traditionally if you were going to order a bunch of product manufactured somewhere else you would have to buy it in bulk. Let's say you found a phone accessory and wanted to sell it as your own product. The manufacture might have 1000 minimum order quantity which might cost you thousands of dollars and it could take two to three months to get! That is valuable time you don't have!

With candles, it is much different. There is usually no minimum order quantity on supplies. You could literally buy enough for only one candle if you wanted. Also you can make the product and have it ready in just a few hours. All of this is super helpful when you are trying to start an efficient business.

WHAT DRIVES YOU?

As mentioned in the first chapter two key points that made me want to start a business to begin with was both freedom of my time and I wanted to be able to do something that I enjoyed doing. For me, this fit the perfect start up also because it allowed me to hit both of those key points in what I was looking for. It is important to analyze what you are looking to do with your business and break success into smaller chunks that are easier to achieve. If your goal is just to make a billion dollars you can see that this target is not able to be complete piece by piece. When your goal is like this it can seem harder to achieve and easier to give up.

WRITE. IT. DOWN.

My suggestion would be to right now get out a note pad and write everything down that you would like to achieve or would like to get from starting your very own candle business. Your list might look something like this:

- Generate enough income a month to pay for rent
- Make side money to afford a vacation
- Sell $5,000 a month
- Make enough to quit my 9-5
- Sell my first 100 candles
- Get candles in a local boutique
- Get a repeat customer
- Sell 10 candles a day

As you begin to grow your business having different goals listed like those above will allow you to check things off and confirm progress. I found that doing this may help you to prevent the break down like I had. Additionally, writing things down makes you more likely to accomplish them, so when in doubt, write it down!

CANDLE BUSINESS TO MILLIONAIRE?

After you have created your list and have bite sized targets, is there money to be made? How difficult is it to achieve some level of financial freedom? How profitable is the candle business? The fact is you can make a lot of money in revenue selling a relatively low number of candles. Since I have been in the candle business I have noticed the average selling price of a candle to be about $28 dollars. At that price per candle you can see why this is the perfect startup. Selling a couple candles a day could completely replace your regular income or just be a great supplement. I know you might want to just know how many candles you have to sell to hit millionaire status, but hold on. Remember what I said? Bite sized pieces.

Let's break down how many candles you would need to sell to reach a level of financial freedom.

Candle Potentials

Before we dive right in and find out what it would take to completely get you to the point of financial freedom where you can ditch the 9-5, let's start when smaller goals.

Let's say you want to go on a vacation and need $800. How many candles would you have to sell to fund your trip?

$28= average candle price
$800/28= about 28 candles!

You would only have to sell about 28 candles to have the $800 for a trip! That is only one candle a day for a month. Not a bad side hustle!

The average American makes between $40,000-$50,000 a year last time I checked, but for this experiment let's say $45,000. Let's find out how much that comes out to a day.

45000/365 days = $123.29 per day!

So now lets say that you have a candle business, and you want to make $123 a day! We will use the average candle price of $28.

123/28= about 4 candles a day! Meaning if you wanted to replace a job income focusing on selling just 4 candles a day! Doesn't sound too bad when you break it down! Not to mention that might only take 30 minutes or your time per day!

What about if you wanted to sell $100,000 a year worth of candles?

$100000/365 days= about $274 a day in sales! How many candles is that?

$274/28= about 10 candles a day!

Now you can see why I got so excited thinking about the potential when looking at creating a candle business and you should be excited too! When you break it down it is easy to see how this idea changed my life and can change yours!

NOT A GET RICH QUICK SCHEME
Now a candle business is not some magic way to become a millionaire literally overnight, however, I have never seen a business that seemed more achievable to become a success. Although I was able to grow my candle business to selling $200,000 a month in a very short time, you must know you don't need to sell hundreds of thousands to do what I would consider well or make a decent living on your own terms. Besides the ability to do well, there is also less risk in my opinion from many other business you could try to start given the low startup cost, ease of

start, and learning to produce product.

You know there is a demand for the product, people have been using candles for hundreds of years and I have no reason to believe that will change anytime soon. Now this doesn't mean you can be just like everyone else. You will still have to differentiate your candles to be something unique and that will make people want to purchase, but if you can make it unique there is a constant demand for the core product itself.

Chapter Takeaways:
- Candle businesses are great start ups when working with a low budget
- Control with producing your own candles allows to be quick and efficient
- Find out what drives your motivation
- Write down bite size goals so you can achieve them one at a time
- Candle price point makes sales level goals achievable when broken down on a per day basis.
- Not a get rich quick scheme, but it can happen!

3. YOU SHOULD ONLY SELL THIS CANDLE

Before we dive into the components that will actually sell you candles and provide you with that irresistible, unique niche that we will talk about in the next chapter, we should learn the process of making candles. Here are my recommendations on where to begin and what to make. There are many types of candles you could make:

- Tapers
- Pillar
- Votives
- Tea lights
- Floaters

- Melts
- Filled candles

It is easy for a beginner to get lost in all these types of candles and not know which one to make. However, if you are looking to start a profitable candle business I have a recommendation for you. I would focus on filled candles. The reason for this is something like a pillar candle , which is a cylinder of wax with no jar, is often very hard to differentiate from other pillar candles and other brands. This makes the candles much more difficult to sell at a premium price because the consumer has no way to justify a high price. I typically see these types of candles competing on one thing, price. Since it is a race to who can be the cheapest this is a very hard method to make any money and I would suggest staying away from these!

The reason I like filled candles so much is the ability to brand your candle and make it unique. There are so many ways to customize a filled candle . These customizations will be what separates you from the competition . These will also be what gives your brand its identity .

CUSTOMIZE YOUR BRAND

- Jar
- Wax type
- Wick type
- Color
- Scents
- Label design
- Lid

- Packaging

These elements will be what separates you from any other candle on the market. I would like you to start thinking of ideas on what your candle might look like, think of maybe candles you like and do not like and make notes of these. It also helps to ask friends and family what they like so you get to see other's specific tastes. I will teach you in the next chapter how to tie all of these together to make a one of a kind candle brand that your customers will fall in love with.

SUPPLIES TO START TODAY!

The most basic supplies to get started today can usually be found right at your local arts and crafts store. I have found you will at first just want to start off with the basics, as you learn how to use these tools then you may get a little more creative with the candle making process. Here are the basics:

1. Pouring Pitcher
2. Saucepan
3. Wax
4. Wicks
5. Hot glue gun or adhesive
6. Fragrance oil
7. Thermometer
8. Small liquid measuring cup or scale
9. Chopsticks or wick holders
10. Warning Label (Caution Label)
11. Coloring (Optional)
12. Label (Optional)

Pouring Pitcher- This metal pouring device is a

must have for any candle maker. This allows you heat your wax to melt it down and also is the perfect pouring device. When using the a pouring pitcher to melt the wax it is also best that you also use a saucepan to prevent the wax from overheating. This is known as the double boiler method.

Wax- There are many types of wax to choose from. I suggest picking a wax that fits the best with your image of what your candle brand will show. For example, there are more eco-friendly options and there is the more traditional styles such as paraffin.

There are three types of waxes that are most commonly used.

- Paraffin Wax- is one of the most commonly used wax in candle making. This is what most of the general candle brands use. It offers an easy pour process and is easier to avoid mistakes when using this wax. It is also very forgiving. However, I have noticed many small candle companies begin to avoid using this material because of the fact that it is a by-product of petroleum. The green community would generally prefer a wax with a cleaner burn, than something based off of petroleum. I have noticed also that paraffin tends to throw a lot of black soot which can darken walls and ceilings.

- Soy wax- this is my personal favorite wax. It has become a high demand as people begin to try to "natural" alternatives. Soy wax is made by using soybean oil, which is believed to be a good sustainable product for candle wax. Soy wax really started making an appearance with candles in the 1990s, but now it is very common. When shopping for soy wax it is important to check what the wax is made of. There are some "soy blends" that can contain paraffin, beeswax, or even palm wax. The 100% soy wax that I used had a lower recommended melting temperature than the 185 degrees that mentioned above, so it is good whether you are using pure soy wax or a blend to double check the melting temperature and the temperature at which you should add the fragrance oil.

- Beeswax- is often a lesser known material for making candles, but surprisingly is one of the oldest materials used to make candles. They had actually discovered beeswax candles in the pyramids, making this one of the oldest methods to make candles. Have you ever seen the combs of a beehive? That is where this wax is extracted from. Beeswax can be purchased in both slab form and pellet form, pellets work great because they melt faster!

Wicks-Surprisingly you do need to buy the correct size. There are MANY different wicks and sizes. You need to be sure to buy the correct wick for your wax. Paraffin and soy wax typically use a different wick. It also depends on the diameter of the jar you choose, wider jars need thicker wicks. Many candle supplies stores online will have an exact guide to direct you with the correct wick to buy if you do not want to use the trial and error method. A good wick will give you a nice even melt pool. A wick to small will often leave un-melted wax on the outside of your candle jar so it is important to make sure you find the correct size.

Fragrance oil- There are almost unlimited scents out there to choose from. When making candles you will notice not all fragrance oils are the same. Some have more scent, some have less. Some do not work well with soy and some do. You really should test these with your product before committing to large amount of scent, you do not want to be left with expensive fragrance oil you can't use! I have found that you can often times buy 1oz samples and are a great inexpensive way to test your scents first!

Thermometer- Is a must have tool in the candle making process. Without this, you will not be melting the wax to the correct temperature to pour or add fragrance oil. If your wax is not at the correct temperature here are a few things that will happen. The wax will have "sink holes" on the top. This is when you have poured the candle and it won't cool correctly because it was poured at the wrong temperature. Your candle will actually have holes in the top or craters and this will not look good. This can be fixed with a hair dryer or a heat gun by reheating the top if this ever happens. Another common issue that your wax could be to cool when pouring and will not adhere to the glass well. While this doesn't usually cause issues when burning, it does not look the best and will affect the quality look to your candles.

Small measuring cup or a scale- Be sure to pick up either of these. It is important to add enough fragrance to your candle without adding to much. As I said above, you want your fragrance to be 3%-10% of the total mixture (oil and wax). A good starting point may be for every pound of wax add 1oz of fragrance oil. If the candle smells to weak, the most I would add is 1.6oz to 1 pound of wax.

Candle Prep:

- The first thing you must do prior to melting the wax is prepping your candles so they are ready to pour once you melt the wax.
- The first thing I always do is flip every candle jar upside down and apply the safety/warning labels on the bottom of the jars. Once I confirm every candle has a warning label I flip all the jars right side up. This way no jar has the possibility of not having a warning label.
- After you apply the warning labels you can insert the wicks. I prefer adhesive stickers designed for candle wicks to stick my wicks to the bottom of the jar. If you do not have these you can use a hot glue gun and stick the wicks to the bottom that way. The problem with hot glue though is that it tends to leave a stringy spider web like glue everywhere and can be a real hassle to clean up.
- Once the wicks are added, I will line up

all the candles in a row to get ready to pour. Before you pour, you need to center the wicks. I use chopsticks, they work great and usually you can buy them in packs of about 300 for very cheap. You just place the chopsticks on top of the glass and place the wick in the middle of the chopsticks. If you would like a different alternative to chopsticks they do sell wick stands that do the same thing as chopsticks, but I have actually found them to not work as well and can be more expensive.

Here are the steps to melting your candle wax:
(Caution! Be careful on these next steps! It does involve boiling water and wax which can be hot and potentially burn you if you are not careful!)

1. Fill a large sauce pan about halfway with water. Move the sauce pan to the stove and begin to heat. Medium to low heat might be a good place to start.

2. Place the desired about of wax in the pouring pitcher. I like to do about half full. This will make pouring the candles much less messy.

3. Move the pouring pitcher to the saucepan. The way I have found that works best is putting the pitcher handle on the edge of the saucepan. This makes it easier to remove in my opinion. Leave the pitcher in the saucepan until all the wax is completely melted. If you notice

some of the water in the sauce pan begins to evaporate, add more water as needed.

4. Whatever wax you use there will be a recommended temperature to pour at and add fragrance oil. Use your thermometer to monitor your wax temperature when melting. Remove the pitcher from the saucepan when you have found your desired temperature.

5. It is now time to add fragrance oil and color if you plan on that. If you are using liquid color, one drop should be enough, if you are using solid brick color, you might want to add one square and then add more if a darker color is desired. With most wax you should add the fragrance oil at around 185 degrees Fahrenheit (check this with thermometer to ensure your wax is the correct temperature). It is always good to double check your own specific wax though to make sure 185 degrees is a good temperature. It is a good rule of thumb that your fragrance oil should be between 3%-10% of the total wax weight. So in a 10oz candle you would aim for anywhere between .48oz of fragrance oil to 1.6oz. You can measure this out using a scale or a small measuring cup. The small measuring cup I use to measure my fragrance oil is only slightly larger than a shot glass and has ounce markings on the side. This is a very handy tool to quickly measure.

6. Once Fragrance oil is added, stir the wax and oil mixture well. Anywhere from 30 seconds to 1 minute should be sufficient. If you ever notice pockets of oil in a finished candle this can usually be fixed by mixing longer. This usually will happen because the wax is not thoroughly mixed with the fragrance oil.

7. If you have added the desired color and fragrance you should be ready to pour! It is helpful to have paper towel ready. Sometimes when using a pitcher to pour wax will run down the edge and drip. The best why I have found to avoid this is quickly wiping the side of the pitcher with your paper towel after each pour.

8. Let each candle cool for at least 6 hours

As with anything else there is a bit of a learning curve when it comes to pouring candles. If you follow each of these steps you should have a straight forward and trouble free process. If you should run into issues make slight tweaks to things like temperature and fragrance oil until you perfect your candles. (Note: it is always a good idea when making candles to keep a fire extinguisher nearby and know to use it. I have thankfully never had to use one, but if a mistake is ever made and you need one, you will be glad you took the precaution.)

Chapter takeaways:

- Though there are many types of candles, I recommend focusing on filled candles for the highest profitability.
- There are many ways to customize your candle with filled candles
- Make sure you have all the supplies needed prior to making candles
- Decide what wax type works best for you
- Don't buy the wrong size wick, your candle will not burn right
- Prep jars first, then melt wax
- Always take safety precautions (including a fire extinguisher)

4. PICKING A NICHE

I was watching my favorite TV show where these business owners go and pitch their idea to investor. It was so fascinating to me. It always seemed like these small companies with products for the most part I have never heard of doing six and seven figures! It amazed me how this was possible when I had never even heard of these products or businesses. For many of them, what was the key? They picked and went after a certain niche.

NICHE > GENERAL
So what is a niche? Basically a niche is a small group of people that have a specific common interest. This

can be used to create a more targeted product for them. Using candles as the example, if you go to any large store, there is generally a candle section. They all usually have the same "big box" store look and are made for the mass audience. They are not a product that is tailored to one specific interest. Picking a niche is not only a way to provide a unique product that interests a customer more, but it also allows you to charge a premium on the product you provide because of its uniqueness.

WHAT NICHES WOULD YOU TARGET?

At this point I want you to think about all the ways you could differentiate you candle business? What are your interests? Where do you see a gap in the candle market? Picking a niche is going to be what is the whole foundation of your candle brand. Once you pick a niche, you need to be laser focused on sticking with that. If you begin to blend a bunch of niches together you slowly become more general and lose you brand value. This is not a good way to add value to the customer. Let's explore some possible niche opportunities:

NICHE OPPROTUNITES

- Green sustainable candle
- Luxury candle
- Funny candle
- Candle for people interested in wilderness
- Candles for men
- Candles for people who like sports
- Candles for pet lovers
- Candle company that has ties with a specific

region
- Gifting candles

Now I could literally go on forever on different niche opportunities, they are literally endless. Think about what interests you. Can you come up with any niche ideas that you think would make a good candle? If so write them down. List all the ways you could customize the candle to fit with the niche you are going after. Let's go through some of these niche opportunities and go over how you might be able to customize each candle to fit the niche.

NICHE: PET LOVERS

Candle For pet lovers- if you were to do a candle brand with this as your niche, you need to start thinking of every possible way you could make this as unique as possible. You want to make something that is different enough that the customer no longer only wants or needs just a candle, but can also connect or be interested in your candle in some other way. Let's look at some ways we could make this very unique. Perhaps you could start with using an animal shaped jar. This doesn't necessarily have to be a specific candle jar. You could use many different things. If you found a dog coffee mug that was shaped as a dogs face, that is an example of something you could use! This makes your product stick out and separates you from the rest of the crowd. You could also create a fun dog label with a custom image of someone's pet. This would be something that could create a great gift for someone. Even if the customer doesn't have pets, it might be something they could give as a gift. Another idea is instead of naming your candle scents traditional things like lavender or apple, you could have scent names as things such as golden retriever hair or purring kitty. To you or I, that might not sound like a desirable candle, but that is the point of picking a niche. We are wanting to narrow the audience and create a stronger connection to the customer, so there is a greater chance of getting a sale compared to a general candle.

NICHE- CANDLE FOR MEN

Another idea could be making a candle targeted for men. I think many times candles are designed with the female consumer in mind. You might notice this in the label design, the scent name, the jar selection, or just you might notice it is being sold in a women's boutique. This presents an opportunity to create a candle for men. If I were to do this I would focus on using bold, masculine fonts on the label. You could make scent names that could be related to more male things, for example, you could have a scent like baseball glove leather or game day scent. Guys like candles too and if you can get them a product that they feel is more tailored to them, you might have a home run!

NICHE- ECO FRIENDLY

It seems like green products and eco-friendly products are quickly becoming more popular. This could be a perfect opportunity to capitalize on the green movement! There are a couple ways I quickly see how you could make a truly "green" candle company. Here are a few ways I think you could focus on the green movement. First, I might think of how we can create the most sustainable jar or what we might be able to put the candle in. Perhaps you could use recycled glasses. These could be antique or maybe use part of an old wine glass. You could talk about how each glass is different because they are all recycled and are helping lead to a cleaner world! I am sure this is something that everyone that cares about the environment might be interested in! You could also use soy wax and explain how it is grown from soy beans and could be considered a more green alternative to the paraffin wax competition. You might even choose to not use a label on your candles and explain that posting your brand on a label is not as important to your company as making a "green" as possible candle. I would, however, find a way to make your candle recognizable. Finally, you could start a whole movement with your candle company. A great way to do this would to donate a percentage of the profits to an organization that will help with an environmental impact. People love to get behind a company with a mission to do more than just sell their product!

NICHE- LOCAL CANDLES

I see local candles as a great opportunity. I also see a few different ways this could be implemented. Today it seems like "local" anything is a huge hit! This could be micro-breweries, local coffee, local fruits and vegetables. People tend to feel a connection with local items and I believe that this leads people to feel inclined to support these local businesses. One way to go after this "local" movement is that you could create a candle brand around the name of your city, state, or region. If it was made in their own city, you might be the next local hit! However, a more scalable strategy might be using local names on a bigger level. The way this might be implemented is if you have a candle scent name of a city that you live or maybe you grew up in. You could do this for tons of cities across the country. Your brand could focus on bringing part of home to where you are now, a symbolic candle of home. For example, someone that might move to New York, but is from Florida might be interested in a "Florida" scented candle. You could make this scent something like ocean breeze so the customer can be reminded of their home state every time they light the candle.

NICHE- FUNNY CANDLES

Funny candles are personally my favorite niche and I will explain why. Picture everyone sitting around some sort of gift exchange. Uncle bob just got a pair of socks and everyone is already looking for the next person to open a gift. I am pretty sure there is nothing less exciting than watching someone open a brand new pair of white socks. Now imagine the next person is about to open their gift and they are going to open a candle, do you think the "big box" candle will get the same reaction as the socks? It might, and this is why it is so important to be different. If that same candle that was opened had a funny scent name, I can almost promise you the reaction will be completely different. Imagine the scent name was dog poop. I am sure the person opening the gift will at least laugh a little at the sight of a dog poop candle, but it's what happens next that is the magic behind niche growth. After the person opening the candle laughs, do you know what happens next? Suddenly everyone's attention is on the candle and what is it that made this person laugh. The person opening it shouts "it's dog poop scent!" and suddenly everyone in the room wants to smell it and see it. At the same time people are passing it around to smell it, people are asking "where is that from?" The people asking are already thinking about who they could get it for because how fun it just looked to give a funny gift.

THE WHOLE PICTURE, YOU MUST SELECT A NICHE

You can see how if you used a niche like any of these examples, it could lead to explosive growth. That first purchase, turns to two purchases, which turns to four purchases and so on. This is exactly what happened in my business that lead and propelled the business into hyper speed sales in just a few months.

Just like the gift example, I want to explain in a different way of the importance of niche and why you must choose one. If you create a candle for people that enjoy the outdoors or for people that like camping, they bought that because that niche is relatable to them. So with that one sale, is that the end of sales? Or does each customer have the potential to turn into a potential promoter for your brand free of charge? When you pick a niche and create a unique product that the customer can enjoy this can happen! Here is what I have seen. The customer might post of on social media out their outdoor adventures or supplies. If they like your product, there is a good chance they could either post a picture of it or it at least be in the background of an image. Sometimes companies will even pay people to do this and it is known as influencer marketing. We are not interested in that right now, but what I am saying is instead of having to pay them, if you product is unique enough for this niche audience, the customer might just post a picture of it because they liked it. Here is why this works so well, each customer is likely to have friends or family interested in the same thing they are. For this example, it is outdoors activities. This means as long as the customer enjoys your product, there is a chance they will tell other potential customers about your products as well. You can see how this could begin to snowball your sales quickly!

Chapter Takeaways:
- Niche is the advantage us smaller candle makers have over the "big box" brands
- Niche IS better than general when starting out
- Pick one niche and stick with it
- Explore your own ideas of possible niche opportunities
- Niche groups can be free promoters of your product
- Niche can create rapid snowball effect growth

5.WHAT SALES CHANNEL IS FOR YOU?

Now we have learned a lot up until this point, you now know what supplies you need, how to make candles, and even learned about different niches. I think you are probably wondering where can I actually sell these items? Now there are really many places you could sell your candles, but we are going to focus on the most tried and true. If you are like me, when I first started out I was doing everything, making candles, marketing, going to art fairs, packaging, designing. You will have to use your time wisely. A good way is to avoid unnecessary distractions and sales methods. There are a few different sales channels that you may be interested in trying. What sales channel do you want? I have broken this down into a few segments and I will list pros and cons of each. At the end I will tell you which sales channel I would suggest and what brought me over $200,000 a month in revenue.

SALES CHANNELS (PROS&CONS)

In store:

Pros:

- Ability to sell candles with little to no advertising cost
- Low cost start up to sell cost, no need for added costs like website hosting

Cons:

- Take less profit
- Less scale, less potential for growth
- Tie up inventory
- Time consuming

Art Shows:

Pros:

- Free and low cost to enter
- Quality traffic
- Networking opportunities

Cons:

- Inconsistent sales
- Dependent on art show
- Time consuming
- Have to invest in booth supplies
- Low Scalability

Direct online store:

Pros:

- Maximum profit potential
- Maximum Growth
- Building an asset
- Control

Cons:
- Can be expensive
- Requires set up time
- Generally you must advertise

Etsy, Amazon, Ebay:
  Pros:
- Free traffic
- Can get views with no advertising
- Easy to follow system to list products

Cons:
- Limited control on traffic
- Limited control on sales
- Could be ranked so far down that no one finds your products
- Commission fees

INSTORE SALES:

It is a common misconception that getting your products into stores is almost an impossible task. While it can be difficult, we are going to cover why you want to get your candles into stores and how to do it!

First I love in store sales because there are many ways to do this very low cost, which is perfect for those just starting out. If you think about the two things you can invest it is time and money. Getting your candles in stores is a low cost, but time commitment. So if you are willing to put in the time, this can be worth it!

When I first started out this was a method I tried in the very beginning and had success with it. I was getting in 40% of the stores I was pitching my candles too! This was a very high rate of success and I will teach you all the steps I did to go and get a success rate of 40%!

The first step I would take is before you enter a single store you must think like the store owner. Why would they want to carry my candle? What do I have to offer them? Will I make this as seamless for them as possible? These are all questions the store owner will be asking themselves while you pitch the idea. It is your job to answer all of those questions before they have the chance to ask them. The reason you do this is because it eliminates many of the excuses they could bring up on why they cannot carry your candle line.

However, while answering all those questions is critical, the most important question you must answer is "why will carrying these candles make me more money?" This will be the main question the store owner will want to know.

So before we talk about the candle aspect of convincing the owner accept to carry it in the store, we must decide how to price it. Traditionally when products are carried in a store the split is 60/40. Let's break this down so you can get a clear picture of how wholesale pricing works:

Wholesale: The store owner actually buys a set

amount of product from you, the candle business owner. You could give larger quantity discounts to incentivize the store owner to buy more. Below is a general rule of thumb to figure out how much to price your wholesale candles.

60/40 Split:
The 60% of the price goes to you the candle business owner , and the 40% goes to the store owner.

$28 candle would work out like this

Candle business owner sells the candle at 60% of the suggested retail price – 60% = $16.80
Store owner profits 40% – 40% =$11.20

As you can see selling in stores can take a bite out of your profit, but the store owner is the one doing all the work to sell! It can be worth it though! Suppose the store sells one candle every other day, that would come out to 15 candles a month! If you are making $16.80 x 15 candles a month, that is about $252 in revenue a month! Now imagine you get in 4 stores that is an extra $1000 a month! You see, investing the time in the beginning to get into stores can really pay off!

This all sounds great, but what do you say if the store owner says something along the lines of they do not have the money to carry the product or do not want to take the risk? This is where you offer to do consignment! Consignment is when you give the product to the store owner and they will try to sell it.

You agree on a set commission and if it sells you get paid for the candle, but you pay the store owner the commission. However , if the candles don't sell the store owner will usually just give the unsold product back to you and no money is lost or gained. This is a way to eliminate the risk for the store owner and allows them to be more willing to test out the product! For this method you, the candle business owner usually will take a little more profit since the store owner is taking less risk. I might suggest 70%-30% , but it is really just is up to you and what you are willing to take and how much margin for profit you have.

While it is important to understand the numbers and how to price candles when they are going it a store, you need to make sure you can picture your candle in that particular store. This comes back to thinking about niche. Every small local store or boutique you go into is going to have its own niche. Make sure that you are only going into stores that have a similar niche as your candle brand.

I have also found it helpful to even set up a display prior to going into stores at your home. Photograph this display and how you envision it looking in a store. This can help the store owner get an idea how to display the candles in their own store. This also presents the opportunity to sell a display with your candles or offer to provide a free display if they order a certain amount of candles from you. It is important to remember that this display should be small. Every square foot is critical for the store owner and maximizing the dollar they can make per square foot is a must! If your display you are showing will take up half the store I do not think they will be interested, so think small!

To wrap up the in store section, I want to quickly explain what niche is my favorite for in store sales! I think this could be of value and might be something you may want to try! My favorite niche for in store sales is local or geographical ties to the area. For example, your candle brand could be named after your city or state. Another idea is you could make the scent names after local geographical areas. For example, you could make a scent name after a local lake, or a scent name after a local state park. I have found that local retailers love to carry local products. Why? Because they sell! This goes back to the microbrewery boom, the eat local movement, etc. The point is people love local things. You can instantly feel more of a connection to a local product and people also love to support other local businesses. If you are interested in selling candles in stores locally, you may want to try this niche!

ART FAIR TIME!:

This is often one of the first places candle business think to sell their product. Art fairs are great and can really help you optimize your products. This is the only place you can have one on one interaction with the customer and find out exactly what they like and what they don't like.

Given that this is a place many candle makers think to sell their candles, can you think of a problem? You got it! The competition can be tough! With usually multiple candle vendors it can be tricky to stick out. However, if you follow the rules of picking a niche, you will often times out sell all of the competition. You see by picking up this book and educating yourself first, you get to skip many of these learning steps that many candle businesses first go through. I have noticed 90% of these candles businesses at these art fairs to not have a niche. They generally have a very general theme with no niche. Think about what the customer wants at an art fair. They want something unique from local artists. If your candle business has a general name and the same old scent names like lavender, vanilla, etc why would they want to buy your candle for $28? They can get a similar general candle at any big box store for $8. This is where I continue to push the importance of picking a niche. This will be the factor that allows you to outsell all the other candle vendors.

Are art fairs profitable? Art fairs require a little more risk since they require a little more upfront investment. Typically you need to invest in supplies and decorations for your booth and also the fee to be a seller at the art fair. I recommend starting out small with art fairs, due to the cost of them. Even though you should go in prepared, the experience of art fairs is something that just needs a little bit of practice. You need to familiarize yourself with talking to potential customers and build the confidence that comes with practice.

I have found that you, your product, or banners need to be able to communicate what is the unique value added in as little as 4 seconds. If you have a funny candle communicate that in 4 seconds, a camping/ outdoors candle? Just 4 seconds! After my experience with art fairs and observing people, I have a very specific reason for this. At art fairs customers often times won't want to browse a booth if they think they are not interested in the product, and if they can't tell what the product is… well then they probably won't be interested in it. From my observations this is because they know if they go to a booth two things usually happen. They get talking to the artist and will feel obligated to purchase or they decide they don't want anything and almost feel guilty for not supporting the artist. This is the reason I believe people will skip your booth. It needs to be communicated well what you are selling. If it is a candle you are selling, the customer has smelled candles before. It is your duty to explain in four seconds why your candle is unique and why the customer should spend the time to come check out your products.

If you communicated that message, well, you probably have people browsing your booth! Fantastic! What if they are ready to buy? What are some of the most important things to consider when you have paying customers to make the most amount of profit as possible? The UP-SELL!

The up-sell is one of the most important tactics of art fairs and many other businesses. Have you ever been to a fast food restaurant and you tell them what you would like? After that they probably ask you if you would like to add fries and a drink to your order for a discount?   This is something that I always noticed the successful booths mastered. The up-sell is basically when someone is ready to purchase, what can you offer them that they will spend more money at your booth. To master the up-sell you need to think like a sales person! However, once I understood the up-sell, I was able to increase my revenue at art fairs by 50%! That is why this is so important! Here are a few up-sell techniques:

- Buy 2 get 1 free
- Gift set
- Wick cutters
- Free surprise gift when you spend $50 or more
- Candle display holder half off with purchase of any candle

These are all items you can offer the customer to try to increase the order value. For example, you could offer a gift set. It could include a custom card, box, and set of matches. Offering something like this you might be able to charge an extra $8 and if it only cost you $2 you just made and extra $6 dollars from the same customer!

So how do you use the up-sell? The best time to offer the upsell is after the customer has already shown intent to purchase. For example, the transaction might go something like this.

You- " Hello! Great choice on the candle! That is my actually my favorite scent! Is there anything else I can help you with"

Customer- "Thank you! I don't think so. This should be it."

You- "Oh I almost forgot to tell you, since you were here on the last day of the art fair, if you purchase one more candle we will give you a third for free!"

Customer- "Oh wow! That would be great! I will take these two!"

You see and just like that the order total went from $28 to $56 AND the customer is happy! This is a perfect example on how to execute the perfect up-sell!

So what is the biggest reason I don't like art fairs? It isn't the upfront investment or the fact they take a little bit of practice. The reason I don't like them is that they are inconsistent. Imagine if your whole business revolved around the art fair with no other sales channels. You might locally have 4-5 art fairs a year. What if it rains for one art fair? What if you are sick for one art fair. The problem is it is very difficult to have a stable business with only attending art fairs as your only sales channel. They are to spread out for your business to have consistent sales. While they can provide an excellent supplement to your business and sales, it is important to have sales channels that can provide more stable results.

ETSY , EBAY , AMAZON:

I would say the second most common place new candle makers start to try to sell candles in places like Etsy, eBay, or Amazon. Now these can be great places to sell and I have actually heard of some Etsy sellers doing great! A wonderful benefit to these is it is often free or very low cost to set up an account and list your products. However, the hard part is there will be thousands of other candles right in front of the same customer. This makes the decision hard, and it could be difficult to even appear in that first 1000 candles. You might be left with little to no views on your candles!

What is the solution here? If you create a niche candle you will have a much better chance of showing up. When creating a listing on these sites you often times will have to enter keywords. This is different than your title. If you were to have an eco-friendly, "green" candle brand you would want to have a description and keywords that focus on eco-friendly related characteristics of your candle.

For example your keywords might be like this:

- Eco-friendly candle
- Sustainable candle
- Recycled Candle
- Green Candle
- Clean burning candle
- Soy wax candle

By adding keywords and descriptions with keyword examples like this your candle has a better chance of appearing in front of customers because you have a more unique and targeted product. You will have a much easier time with these specific properties to show up in a search, than if you were just to have a general vanilla scented candle.

Now, if you successful and are able to attract customers with keywords and get sales, these marketplaces have to make money somehow. Often times this is in the form of a commission on each sale. This generally isn't an issue if you have enough room for profit, but you want to make sure you calculate all the fees and commission before setting your listing price. These fees and commissions could prevent you from having profit and actually lose money on a sale!

Here is how to check if you are still profitable

(PRICE SOLD x (1-COMMISION)) – COST OF PRODUCT= PROFIT

For example:
If you sold one candle for $28 and you get charged 30% commission. How much profit will you make if your candle cost $10 to make?

(28 x (1-.30)) – 10= $9.60

Profit $9.60

In this scenario you would have made profit, but you must be careful to do that math before listing your item to make sure you will make a profit!

While I have listed the pros and cons about online marketplaces, the biggest disadvantage is the competition. Even if you are able to appear under eco-friendly candles, there is nothing stopping someone else from copying every part of your candle. This often times can end in a price war which is not good. A competitor lowers their price by a dollar, you lower your price a dollar. This continues until both you and your competitor are only making pennies per sale vs 10+ dollars. So what do you do if you still want to sell online but want to ditch the online marketplaces?

HANDS DOWN BEST SALES CHANNEL...
The absolute best sales channel is your own website. Sometimes this can sound a bit intimidating to someone who has never done it before, but it is a very effective method with the biggest upside potential. Let me explain the benefits, you own the website.

Owning the website and brand is critical! You control all the aspects of the website! Having a website is literally like having a real store that someone can go to 24/7 365 days a year! When you sell something you don't get charged a commission, you keep all the profit!

Your website can be relatively cheap to run and operate and can even automate many of the tasks for you! This will also give all your customers a place to return and see all your updates and place new orders! This will help that snowball effect I had just mentioned!

One thing that people often see as a down side is generally you must advertise in some way for your website. This can be a very intimidating thing especially if you think only the big brands have money for that. I want to help get rid of that idea that only the large corporations can advertise and how you can get a piece of that pie too! You can start advertising for as little as one dollar a day!

In the next chapter I will explain how you can create your own website to start getting sales today!

Chapter Takeaways:
- There are many different sales channels you can use
- Niche will almost always help each sales channel you are in
- Be careful commissions and fees don't make your product unprofitable
- Owning your own website has significant advantages
- Do not be afraid of the word "advertising"

6. BUILDING A WEBSITE THAT SELLS

So you have decided you want to make a website! My goal is to take you step by step through this process to get your site up and running quickly! I promise it is not as hard as it sounds! Having a website is a key asset to your candle brand and will give you the possibility to make money while you sleep! Having your own website is a great thing!

Before you begin you should have a grasp on what your candle niche is and at least have a prototype created. If you get to that point, you are ready to start thinking about starting a website.

Something I want you to understand is I am about to walk you through exactly how I built my candle business that was able to generate $200,000 a month. I am going to be will not be leaving anything and will explain how fast you could be set up and selling today. If you have your niche and your prototype you could even be ready to sell within 30 minutes of finishing this chapter!

Ok so where do you even begin? I use website called Shopify to create my websites and I would recommend this for you too! Shopify is a great all in one tool. They manage your inventory, create simple drag and drop features to make creating a website a breeze . They even manage all your orders and allow you to create shipping labels right from one platform! It makes creating a website so much easier than it was years ago.

LETS BUILD THIS THING!

The first step would be to go over to shopify.com and create and account. This can be done in as little as 30 seconds. At the time of writing this book, they even offer a free 14 day trial, so hopefully you are able to take advantage of that!

Step 1: Once you make an account, you should get brought to a screen that prompts you with the first steps to take like this page.

It tells us that we should add a product, customize theme, and add domain. These are the main steps you will need to take and once you complete these your store will be live!

We are going to go over how to optimize each step so you can turn every visitor into a sale!

ADDING A PRODUCT

When you add a product there are a couple things you must customize! These include:

- Title
- Product description
- Images
- Price
- Shipping weight
- Inventory (optional)

I would say at a bare minimum make sure that you edit all of these to be sure your customers are well informed of your product and that the billing for shipping is correct.

TITLE:

How important is the title? It is very important for two reasons. To communicate to the customer on what your product is and to allow customers to find you with SEO (search engine optimization). Creating a compelling title is important, if something was titled "Candle" or "Fresh Outdoor Pine | Soy wax Camping Candle | 40 hour burn time" what do you think sounds more compelling to a customer? Of course, the longer more descriptive title! I have found a good method for title creation and this is done by breaking the title in three segments. The first segment is the title of the candle name or scent, and the second and third are broken down into product features. I would pick the most two important and list them there. As you can see in the listing I used "soy wax camping candle" and "40 hour burn time" this was so that the customer knows what it is, what and who it is for, and how long will it last.

The title is also important for SEO. This essentially means that your website could show up if those keywords are typed into a search engine. If I were to type in "soy wax camping candle" on the internet, your candle and website might pop up and this can drive traffic directly to your site for people looking for a product just like what you have.

DESCRIPTION:

Next you have to list a description. This is important and needs to answer all the questions the customer might have. If their question is not answered it can turn into a lost sale! Have as much information in your description so that does not happen! Here is an example of a good description:

CANDLE SPECIFICATIONS:

About: Hand poured in USA, Cruelty Free, using only the highest quality ingredients.

Scent notes: Lavender, vanilla, apple

Wax: We use only premium soy wax. This provides a much cleaner burn than other paraffin(petroleum) based candles. Also, soy wax provides a much longer lasting burn!

Wick: We use only lead and zinc free wicks.

Scent: Quality and satisfaction are our number one goal. We use our own unique blend of only the highest quality fragrances available. This will provide you with the best aroma experience possible.

Net weight: 12oz

Shipping Speed: All candles are shipping USPS Priority Mail. This mail service is typically 2-3 Days.

You can see how this looks not only clean, but answers all the questions as quickly as possible. Depending on what your candle is you may need to add features to the description to make to applicable to the product you are selling.

IMAGE:

Product Photography does not need to be complicated! I tend to think the simpler the better. I have illustrated below how you can create beautiful pictures for literally under $2. All you need is a camera or smartphone and two pieces of white poster board paper.

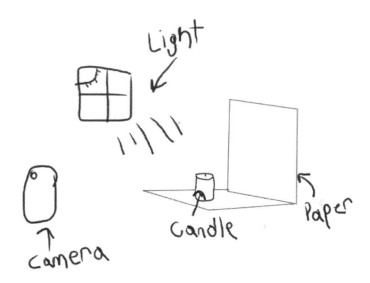

Set up should go like this. Find any table and place one of the poster boards on top of the table. Then back that table up to a wall preferably next to a window with good sunlight coming through. Place the other poster board on the wall so it is the background for the image. That is it! This will provide a clean cut white background for you candle! Also what I like to sometimes do is make each background a little more customized for each scent. I would go to a local craft store and pick out some background features that are specific to each candle scent you have. This is a way to differentiate and make each picture pop out a little more!

Practice is important with product photography! The more you try, the better you will become! So make sure to try many different angles and ask friends and family what image variation they like better! With many aspects of business, it is important to get many different opinions so you know what potential customers might be thinking!

PRICING:

As we briefly covered in an early chapter, the average price of a candle is about $28. Starting out I would recommend starting around this price. Pricing is interesting because it is something you can adjust every few days to see how customers react. For example if you list it for $24.99 you might sell twice as many candles than if you had it listed for $28. In that case lowering the price might be a good. What about if you had a luxury candle and you raised the price to $45 and found out when you raised the price you actually sold more candles than when it was listed for $28. This is why price can be so interesting and is actually a real example I saw before. For that particular luxury candle, it was in higher demand when the price was higher because the perceived value of the candle was higher. In simple terms, people thought that if they paid more, they would actually get a better candle and would enjoy it more. This is the same concept that big companies use with designer handbags. The customer values the purse more simply for the fact that is cost more. The lesson to learn from this is when you are pricing your candle, don't assume you know the magic number. Test different price points to see which one works best with your brand.

SHIPPING & SHIPPING WEIGHT:

The final thing you are going to want to update when adding your product to your online store is the shipping weight. This is important because if you have the wrong weight as the shipping weight you might have to end up paying extra postage fees or even the mail service refusing to mail the package all together! With my online candle store I had it set so the customer paid the shipping. If you go to the settings -> shipping on the Shopify dashboard you can customize how you would like to set up shipping.

Important things to note when it comes to shipping. I had always found USPS to be the cheapest method of shipping. You can use USPS first class for packages under a pound. This is the cheapest service and I found ranges from about $3-$6 which can vary depending on the exact weight and destination. The other option is USPS Priority Mail, which can be used for packages over a pound. I have found the prices for this to vary from $6-$12 but can change with weight of heavier packages.

Now you might be wondering why it is important to know price ranges for shipping rates, but it is very important to understand when the customer is paying for shipping. If the customer sees the candle for $28 they might be willing to buy the candle and proceed to checkout. They just enter all of their information and then all of the sudden, BOOM! They are hit with an unexpected shipping charge. This added charge brought your candle from $28 to $38 and suddenly this is too much for the customer and they decide to leave your website without purchasing anything. This can be a huge issue, but if you notice this is happening, there are a few ways around it. The first suggestion would be to discount shipping. This means you take a set amount of the shipping so it is less of a surprise to the customer. This can be done right on Shopify by using a fixed amount or a fixed percentage. If you were willing to pay for $4 dollars of that shipping in the last example that would mean that customer would have only owed $6. Maybe $6 wouldn't have been as bad as $10 and perhaps they would have continued with their order. You would have had to take a hit to your profit, but perhaps getting the sale vs not getting the sale would have been worth the $4 hit to you profit. Another technique I have found to work well if the shipping is too much for the customer is just find out what your average shipping cost is. For me it was about $8 on a 2 pound package. Once you find this cost you just fix it into the price of the candle. For example, if your candle is $28 just add the $8 into the price of the candle. This would make the new price of the candle $36 and offer free shipping. That might sound like a lot, but when it comes to purchasing things online customers they are used to "free shipping" and when they feel like that have to pay extra for shipping it can be hard to accept. When you fix it into the price the customer feels like the whole $36 is just for the candle but they are actually also paying for shipping.

There is no one answer to know which one will work best for your online store. You will have to test each option to see which one your customers respond the best too.

PRODUCT IS SET UP, NOW WHAT?

Once you have your product set up, you are ready to add a few design elements to your website. This is why I suggest you try Shopify. They make it so easy to customize your own website. From your dashboard you simply go to Online store -> Customize and you will be brought to your online store. They have many things you can add right to your store simply using a drag and drop method. I often times see new websites that create way to complicated of a home screen which leads to confused customers that end up leaving. Here is a basic format you might want to follow that worked well for my store.

- Announcement Bar
- Main Banner
- Products
- Testimonials
- News Letter Sign Up

Your home page can really be that simple and I would suggest starting out trying something similar to that line up. I think it would be beneficial to explain how I used each of these to turn website visitors into paying customers!

The announcement bar is very simple. Have you ever been to a website and there is a very small box across the top? It might say free shipping on orders over $50, or promote a current sale. This is the announcement bar and is perfect for letting your customers know why right now is a perfect time to buy! One announcement text that always worked well for me was letting customers know there was a limited time sale going and it was their last chance to get a 20% discount!

The main banner is the main image you first see when you go to certain websites. Using this banner can be a great way to communicate to potential customers about your brand and the niche. Use this space to really show the niche you are in and the message and feeling you want behind your candle brand. For example if you want an outdoor inspired candle brand maybe you want to go outside and photograph your candle up against some fallen leaves that have nice hints of yellow and red. Or you could photograph your candle with a campfire in the background. What about an eco-friendly candle? I might photography my candle on a desk with a very simply background. I might put a small desk plant with green leaves behind the candle, but I would try to keep it very simple. Think of this banner as you would if you owned a brick and mortar retail location. You wouldn't have a store with one table with candles and no decorations to let everyone know about your brand and your brand image. This is exactly what your banner should be, away to add decorations to your online store.

Once you add the banner I would just add the products in a grid fashion so that your customers can begin looking at your products right away. Don't feel like you need hundreds of products here to have a complete store. I started my store with only 6 products (candle scents). You don't need to do anything specific here. There will be a simple drag and drop when you are customizing your website to display all the candles on the home page.

If you can imagine the process of a new visitor coming to your website, you are trying to sell them on your candle brand. This is why I like to display testimonials right after the products to let the potential customer know that others have enjoyed their candle experience from your brand. It might be a good idea to give a few of your candles away in the beginning in exchange for honest reviews so you have great testimonials to display! This concept is called "social proof" which basically means there is less friction for the customer to purchase due to the fact they can see others have already enjoyed it.

Finally, the perfect ending to your home page is a great newsletter sign up! You can promote this section as a way for customers to find out about sales and upcoming new products. This section can be very valuable because you can collect customers and potential customers emails to then later email market to them with sales and other great promotions you are hosting.

FINISHED HOME PAGE, DO I NEED ANYTHING ELSE?

Awesome job if you completed your home page and made it to this section! There is one last thing I would recommend before making your store live! So right now you will have two pages and if you have added the product page to the navigation menu on your website you will want to add one more page. This should be a "contact us" page. You need to have a way for customers to be able to reach out with any questions, comments, or concerns they might have. A contact us page is a great way to do this!

WHAT DO YOU DO IF YOU NEED

HELP BUILDING YOUR WEBSITE?

While I will do my best through this book to give you proper instruction on how to design a website that sells, there will always be little issues that could leave you not knowing how to change or fix it. In this case what do you do? Another great reason why I love Shopify! They will be happy to help you 24/7 365 days a year! I can't tell you how many times when I first started building my website when I got stuck and frustrated. I was always able to overcome my problems by simply reaching out to the support team. This is a huge benefit when you are just starting out building a website for the first time compared to other website building platforms that do not offer this kind of help.

COMPLEX WEBSITE DESIGN MADE EASY

The last thing I have to say that is a HUGE benefit to Shopify is their diverse app store for custom website applications. This app store is to add custom features to your website without having to pay custom coders thousands of dollars! This feature alone will save you so much money. The great part is there is literally an app to do whatever you would like with your website. The options are endless and they are usually also a simple drag and drop. Once you complete your website I would definitely recommend checking out the Shopify app store to see if there are any additional features you would like to add to your store.

Chapter Takeaways:

- Create a compelling product description that answers any possible customer questions
- Properly set up shipping weight of your candle
- Test different price points
- Think of your online store of an actual brick and mortar store when designing
- It might be a good idea to give away a few free candles in the beginning to get reviews to display
- Shopify makes website creation easy with great support

7. ADVERTISE LIKE A PRO

What do you do now that you have your beautiful website completed? You need to find ways to drive traffic to your website! For myself and others first starting in ecommerce this can sound like a very difficult and expensive task! I am here to explain it does not need to be! You can literally start advertising for free using more time consuming methods or paid methods for as little as $2 a day! There are a few ways of advertising that are extremely cost effective when starting your candle company! Below are the methods I used to grow my candle company!

Advertising Methods:
- Influencer marketing

- Paid promotions & Bloggers
- Facebook Advertising

Influencer marketing- This strategy can be free or even just the cost of a candle! It is can also be a good way to start because similar to art fairs, this generally will allow to you see what potential customers think of your products through comments. What I would do when using influencer marketing is take out a piece of paper and think of all the social media sites there are. Facebook, Instagram, SnapChat Twitter, Pinterest, etc. On all of these platforms there are people literally obsessed with candles, and even people who build their social media around candles. These people are generally followed by people with similar interests. So with that paper we are going to write down all the potential people we can find that have a passion for candles. A good way to find them for example is if we were looking on Instagram we would search for the #candles or maybe search a hashtag of popular candle brands. You will be able to find thousands of people who love candles! I would go through all the profiles and find what profiles look the most focused around candles. These are the profiles you are going to want to write down. Once you have 50-100 profiles you will then go back and message each of these people and ask them if they would like a free candle in exchange to post with your candle! I might reach out with a message like this:

"Hello _____! My name is _____ from _____ candle company. I recently came across your profile and I couldn't help but notice all of your candle pictures! I love to connect with those who share a similar passion that I have! Can I ask a quick favor? I would love you send you a free candle to add to your collection! I would really appreciate it if you enjoyed my candle to mention my company in an Instagram post! Please let me know if you would like to collaborate and I would be happy to send you a candle! Thank you for your time, _____!"

For many of these people they will love the opportunity to not only be noticed by candle companies like yours, but to get a free candle! Now this person might have 200 followers or 20,000 followers, but each follower is a potential customer. So here is what you need to then ask this influencer to do in their post. You must politely ask them that you would really appreciate it if they could tag the candle in the photo and also mention you candle company in the comment. If they do both of these things all of their followers will quickly be able to find your profile. It is your job to turn these people into website visitors once they visit your profile. Here is what I would do to turn all those people who then visit your social media into website visitors. It comes down to your bio, and you need two things in your bio. A reason to shop, this could be something like mentioning a current sale you are running, so you let them know why right now is a good time to visit your shop. It also needs to include your website link or a button to your website. I usually would put this at the very bottom of the bio. Imagine if all these potential customers came to view your profile, but could not figure out a way to purchase. Do not forget to do this prior to having an influencer post with your product!

Paid Promotion & Blogger:

Paid promotion and bloggers are what I would consider to be the same thing as an influencer, but I have separated the two due to the fact that with these paid methods usually a free candle will not be enough for the promotion. You will have to pay these people for a promotion of your brand, but you will most likely be getting your product in front of a larger audience and sometimes a more targeted audience. These people will often times be running these types of promotions for businesses full time as their source of income, so this is why is there is generally a price to pay. If you want to find these types of influencers I might start by viewing blogs. The great thing about blogs is they have the ability to provide a more consistent flow of customers. If that blog post is left up on the blogging website, that could continue to drive traffic to your website months after the original date of the post.

What type of influencers to use for paid promotion and blogs? The benefit to these methods is that just like you and your candle company has a niche, these people generally have their own niche. Since these influencers have a laser focused niche of their own, this is why it can be well worth the money spent. For example if you have an outdoor focused candle company, you could reach out to hiking or camping blogs. If you have a very sustainable, eco-friendly candle company, you could reach out to vegan eating or green living blogs. These are just a few ideas, but you can see if the influencer has a more targeted audience like a niche, you can have influencers besides just those of people who are interested in candles.

So what is a typical price to pay for paid promotion? Whether they have a blog, a YouTube channel, or other social media, there is generally a way to see the reach of these influencers. Some experienced influencers will have what is called a media kit. This generally shows you how much reach they have and what the demographics of their audience is. Not all will have this so do not worry if they do not. If you can get the information on their reach a standard rule of thumb is $7 per 1000 people reached. So if they have 10,000 followers on Instagram, you might have to pay them $70 dollars for a promotion. If you do the math you can quickly see how this can become well worth the money spent. In this hypothetical situation you can see how the payoff and risk with this method can be well worth the risk. Out of the 10,000 people you reach only three people would have to purchase one candle for you to make your money back from the promotion. What else do you get from this also? You continue to grow your brand, besides sales you will gain social media followers and people will begin to share your brand with others also. This is when the snowball begins to roll down the hill and your massive growth can begin.

When starting out with these paid promotions I urge you to start slow, you could have promoters of the wrong niche compared to what you thought promoting your company would resonate with. If using social media, I would suggest maybe influencers with 10,000-50,000 might be a good place to start. If bloggers is what you are looking at doing, start with the people that appear to have good engagement in the form of comments and a close social community, smaller blogs are ok because usually they have an audience that feels more connected to what is going on!

FACEBOOK ADVERTISING:

This is my favorite place to advertise due to the fact that it is extremely scalable! What does that mean exactly? This means that once you are able to find your ad that works, you can simply spend more money and get more results or purchases. Now in the beginning, remember when I was really struggling and things were not working out at all? I had no idea how to drive traffic to my website. I was wasting money on Facebook ads because I had no idea how to target the customer I was actually looking for. Facebook advertising can be a wonderful tool if you use it correctly and a money pit if you do not. It is my goal to teach you all my tricks and tips to growing a successful Facebook advertising campaign to grow your business. Here is an example of after I learned how to properly use Facebook ads, how I was able to scale my candle business and how you can too!

Starting budget $10 a day in advertising. After a few weeks of tweaking my ad I started to consistently get 1-2 sales a day from that advertising budget. On average this was coming out to about $42 in revenue a day from a budget $10! I was very excited! What I soon realized is with every sale Facebook was learning where to show my ad for maximum return on investment. So how did I scale? I just raised my advertising budget. It went something like this:

$10 Ad spend=$42 in Sales
$20 Ad spend=$84 in Sales
$50 Ad Spend=$210 in Sales
$100 Ad Spend=$420 in Sales
$1000 Ad Spend=$4200 in Sales

The wonderful thing is at this point my problem was no longer how to I get sales, sales were flying in! It was how can I make, package, and ship these candles to keep up with demand. This was a wonderful problem to have! This was the point where I was thankful to have friends around that were able to help the fulfillment process of candle making. I even had to get a storage unit to store inventory because I was running out of space!

So how did I get to this point and how can you too? By mastering Facebook advertising. Let's begin to dive into all the secrets with how we can master your Facebook advertising campaigns. We are going to break this down into sections, the goal is to understand each section well and then implement them on your own. If you feel comfortable with all of these sections, remember you can start with very small budget to see how your campaigns are likely to perform.

- Demographic Research
- Pixel, what is it?
- Setting up campaign
- Create Targeting
- Set up Compelling ad
- A/B test

DEMOGRAPHIC RESEARCH:

The first step before you even begin to create any Facebook advertising or actually any advertising for that matter is to make sure you have a very good idea of who your target audience is. You need to understand a good basic foundation of age, gender, interests, and product tastes. This be done with a little recon research as I like to call it. It is pretty simple to do and costs nothing! What I would do is find what I would consider similar products or products in a similar niche. You then need to go on social media sites like Facebook and Instagram and look these products up and find the company pages. You can see everyone who is following that page, everyone who comments or likes their posts, or even who has tagged that company in a post! These are all people that you need to consider in a similar demographic to your company. What you need to do is go through as many of these profiles (followers of a company in the same niche as yours) and start to compile data on a note pad of similarities you notice when looking at all of these people. I would make notes of estimated ages, what is the most common gender, etc. Make notes of anything you can! Once you go through many profiles, the more the better, generalize the information into the "target audience". This will be the group you think is most likely interested in your product. This recon data will be what you use to begin your ad targeting after we set up the Facebook campaign.

PIXEL:

What in the world is a pixel? It is basically a code that allows you to track your ads performance. Ok, so I know that sounds really complicated, especially since all of this is so new but it really isn't let me explain how you set this up. First you will need to create an advertising account and a business page on Facebook prior to doing this. A Facebook page can be easily set up from your home screen once you are logged on to Facebook. You should see something like "create a page" that is where you go to create a page for your business. Once you create a business page you should be ready to set up an ad account. The specific website could change, so the best way to find the set up an advertising account should be just quickly searching on the internet something like "Facebook Ads" This should bring you to the Facebook website where an advertising account can be created. It is very simple to create an account and you should be ready to start creating your campaigns in just a few minutes! Once your actual Facebook advertising account is created it should be time to set up your pixel. You may have to dig around a little bit to find this, but if you go to the settings of your new advertising account you should find something that says Pixel or Pixels. You will to click the button that says create Pixel. Once you create the Pixel you need to copy the code you are given. This is just in the form of a long number. With the Pixel code copied go back to your Shopify dashboard. Remember if you are having trouble finding this next step on Shopify, you can always reach out to the Shopify support team and they can help you locate it! However, if you follow this, you should be able to find it. At the dashboard click "online store"➔ "Preferences." Once you have clicked preferences there should be a spot that says "pixel" and this will be where you paste your pixel code.

Pat yourself on the back! You should have just successfully set up your Pixel! Now go back to your Facebook ad account on the Pixel page where you left off. There should be a spot where you see something along the lines of "test pixel". What this will do is send traffic to your website and make sure that your Facebook ad account is communicating properly! If they are, you will now be able to measure the effectiveness of your adds and allow Facebook to optimize the effectiveness of each campaign. The optimization is important because to my understanding this is how Facebook will learn for you, so you are able to get the best bang for your buck!

SETTING UP CAMPAIGN:

This can be the most confusing section so I will try to make it as simple as possible! I have found that it helps to follow these steps while on the actual advertising dashboard because then you can see exactly what I am talking about and it will make a lot more sense!

Here is how I would set up a campaign and what steps you can take if this is your first campaign too! From the Facebook advertising dashboard you can select create new campaign.

From there you select your marketing objective. This is basically what is your goal you would like to achieve. You can do things like brand awareness, traffic, engagement, conversions, or store visits. The most important objective that you will probably end up using the most is conversions. The word conversions basically means a website purchase or whatever your conversion event is set to. You can have a conversion event set to "add to cart", "initiate checkout", "purchase", etc. This will be the goal you want to achieve and if that goal is achieved it will be considered a conversion.

Where to start? I have found it worked best when I started with the marketing objective of "traffic" and the reason is at first you want people just to go to your website so you can allow that pixel to gather data. This way you can later optimize. When would I switch to conversions as a marketing objective? I would recommend switching once you have 50 conversion events in a week. Where do you check conversion events? You can check that in the pixel section of your advertising account. The first conversion event you will probably have 50 records for is "view content" if you checked this and you do have 50 events for "view content" it might be time to switch from "traffic" to (conversions then under conversions you would select view content) if you don't select view content this is the same section where you have the option to optimize for purchase or add to cart instead. Once you get 50 records for any of these conversion event you can switch, the end goal should be getting 50 conversion events for "purchase" and then optimizing for purchases. That is likely when your campaigns will have the best results. This is what your conversion event section might look like after you start getting traffic and purchases and this is where you select what was just mentioned:

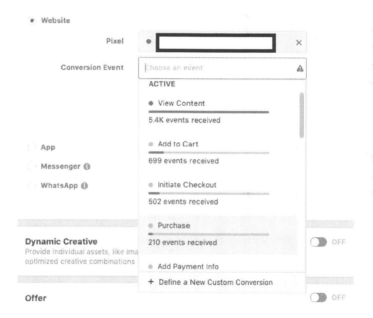

After you select the conversion event you want you will be prompted to select the targeting of your ad. This next figure will show you what possible targeting methods you have available. This is where you can take all the information you gathered during your recon and apply it! Look at all these targeting options we have !

Audience
Define who you want to see your ads. Learn more.

Create New   Use a Saved Audience ▼

Custom Audiences ❶   [Add a previously created Custom or Lookalike Audience]

Exclude | Create New ▼

Locations ❶   [Everyone in this location ▼]

United States

📍 **United States**

📍 Include ▼ | Type to add more locations | **Browse**

Add Locations in Bulk

Age ❶   [18 ▼] - [65+ ▼]

Gender ❶   [**All** | Men | Women]

Languages ❶   [Enter a language...]

Detailed Targeting ❶   INCLUDE people who match at least ONE of the following
❶

[Add demographics, interests o... | Suggestions | **Browse**]

Exclude People

✓ Expand interests when it may improve performance at a
lower cost per result. ❶

We can target based on characteristics like:
- Age
- Gender
- What Language they speak
- Detailed Targeting

This is where you can test the audience you found from you research. If you found most people seemed to people seemed to be male or female, you can select that. What age? If you estimate the age to be 25-35 you can select that also! The point of all of this is trying to get your ad only seen by the people that are most likely to purchase it!

This next section called detailed targeting. It can be very useful! It allows you to select a group of people that are already interested in something and show your ad to only them:

As you can see above I selected people who are interested in candles. That gives me a group of 28,000,000 people to show my ad too that I already know are interested in candles! What else could you select for interests to make your targeting? You could select interests similar to your niche, which is why it is important to have a good idea of your niche and even other companies in that niche. You see if you were to have an outdoor inspired candle brand what could your potential detail targeting options look like?

People who have interests in:

- Outdoor parks

- Hiking
- Other outdoor companies
- Camping

There are so many options you have for targeting people within the niche you choose. This can be such an effective marketing strategy because you are able to show your ad to people you already know might be interested in your ad. Compare this to the traditional types of advertising where you were not able to select a specific market like this.

The best idea is to try a couple at a time by selecting different targeting methods to find on what works best with the ad you have created. What I mean by this is you might want to try setting up a few different campaigns and within each campaign try different detailed targeting. Perhaps if you tried those different detailed targeting groups we just talked about, maybe the hiking audience ends up liking the ad and product more than the camping audience. The only way to find out is to test each group.

AD CREATION:

Once you have completed the targeting you are almost done! Now you just have to create your ad! This part should be pretty easy, it will just take a little bit of creativity!

First you will be prompted with identity. This is just means select the page or profile you want to post the ad for you. You will probably want to select the business page you have just created. Once you select what page or profile is publishing the ad, you will be prompted with selecting what type of ad (Format). I have always found single image or video to work best with my candle business, but I recommend experimenting with each different type of format because what worked best for my candle business, could be different from yours. However, which one you choose the ad creation process is pretty similar. Here are the things you must create:

- Text
- Image/Video
- Headline
- Link
- Call to Action

Text: The text is the section where you can inform the customer about your company. I also liked starting with a question. I found it to grab the attention of someone better. For example, you might start out with something like "Did you know our jars are made from 100% recycled material?". This grabs the attention of someone and can make them interested in learning more about your company. I then would use 3-4 lines giving both key features and a reason to buy right now. Here is what you might want your full text section to look like:

(Did you know are jars are made from 100% recycled material?

We only use eco-friendly soy wax

Made in USA

Shop now because sale ends today!)

Do you see how that is short and sweet? I would tend to avoid cramming paragraphs there because you want to leave a little unknown so they want to click the ad to find out more. A rule of thumb, I always would have some reason to complete purchase now. You want to create an urge of action being taken.

Think about the last time you went to a retail store or drove past that furniture store that has had the going out of business sale for 5 years now. The point is sales have been shown to increase the customer completing a purchase and is something you are going to want to consider with your ad and your actual online store.

Image/Video: Remember taking all those product photos and that diagram I set up to show you how to create a photo booth for your products for just a few dollars? It might be time to bring that back out again. This image or video should highlight your brand and should somehow represent your brand and niche together. It might also be a good idea to show multiple products in your product line. This picture could even be the banner image you used on your website if you would like it to be! It just is important this image can almost explain your brand without reading any of the text if someone saw your ad. You might want to shop around your local craft store for decorations to put in the back ground of this image! Do not worry your first picture will not be perfect, just make sure you continue to master this skill! It always helps if you have a photographer friend! You could ask them for advice and help in exchange for a candle!

Headline: This section needs to be just a few words, probably 8 or less. This needs to be whatever you think the best feature is, why someone should buy your candle, who the candle is for, or even what makes your candle different.

Here are a few examples of headline ideas:

- Eco-Friendly, small batch candles
- Like camping? You will love this candle!
- Your husband will love this candle made just for dudes!
- This candle will remind you of home
- This will be the only candle you ever buy again

These are just a few ideas of headlines, but they all either create interest or quickly explain who the candle is for. This is what you are looking for! What I would do is write 20 different headline ideas on flash cards. Ask anyone you know what the most interesting headline is or what catches their eye the most. This way you can get multiple opinions and that way your idea isn't skewed based on just your own opinion.

Link: This is pretty straight forward. This will be the destination that the customer will get to if they click your ad. I would always send the customer to the home page of my website but you may want to try other things like sending them to the specific product page instead. I might suggest sending them to the specific product page if you are advertising a particular scent in your advertisement.

Call to action: The call to action is the objective that the customer is looking for. Are you trying to educate the customer? Then you might have a call to action of "learn more". Are you trying to have the customer shop and buy a candle? Then you might want to have a call to action of "shop now". This really just depends on what you or the customer wants to achieve by clicking the advertisement. Typically in the ads I used I would always you "shop now" so that the customer knows they are being redirected to an online store.

AD COMPLETED:

At this point your ad should be close to finishing, not finished! If you wanted to publish the ad and start advertising it is as easy as just clicking publish! It may be a good idea before you start to advertise to double check the whole campaign to make sure everything is set up right and how you wanted. I also suggest you check your daily ad budget again, that way you don't end up spending more or less than you wanted.

ADDITIONAL INFORMATION:

Relevancy Score: Once you create your candle ad, your ad will get what is similar to a grade from Facebook. This will be on a scale from 1-10. This scale is called relevancy score and basically shows how relevant your ad is the too people that are seeing it! You should have the goal of making it to a relevancy score of 10! When you get closer to a score of 10, your ad will get better results and usually you will get more traffic, engagement, or purchases with a better score. The daily budget will go much farther on a relevancy score of 10 than it would on an ad with a relevancy score of 5. You can find your relevancy score under the "ad set" section of your campaign.

Advanced Targeting: Once you gain some traffic to your site this when you can really unlock the power of

Facebook ads. This is done by using a look alike audience. A look alike audience is a custom audience that finds people most similar to people who have already viewed your website, made purchases, added to cart, etc. This can be very powerful in making your audience that much more accurate! Imagine being able to show your ad to people just like all your other customers! This feature is amazing ! To create a look alike audience you will go back to the targeting page or audience page of your campaign on the Facebook ad account. Under audience you will select create new → look alike audience. You then can select what you would like to create the look alike audience from. My rule of thumb is to on create the look alike for something you have more than 300 pixel records for. This means if you have 300 records of people visiting your site, but 3 purchases. I would create the look alike audience from the website visitors instead of the purchase records. At the look alike creation page, if you are creating it based on your pixel data, it should tell you how many records there are for each option.

If you are about to create a look alike audience you will be given a 1%-10% to choose from. If you choose 1% that will be the 1% of the people most similar to who you are trying to target. I always found that 1% worked best for my campaigns. This will now be a great targeting method. If you wanted you could even try removing the detailed targeting like "camping" or whatever you used for your candle company and just try using the look alike audience. For me, I found it worked best removing the detailed targeting and just using a look alike audience.

FACEBOOK ADVERTISING CONCLUSION:

This section of the book probably seems like a TON of information. It can be discouraging when getting to this advertising section and learning about something that just sounds like a new language more than anything else, however, it isn't that scary. If you follow these step while in the Facebook ads dashboard, you should be able to navigate pretty easily! The platform itself appears to be designed in a straight forward way that can help avoid confusion when just starting out! However, while you work through Facebook ads you will discover more advanced features. That are beyond the scope of this book. That being said, I do not believe they are absolutely necessary when just starting out. In fact, the only features I used in my candle business are the features that I taught you how to use. Facebook ads, like everything else in the candle business has a learning curve. You need to just understand that your first campaign might not be a home run, but that every step of the way you commit to learning more and crafting your skills. If you focus on continuous improvement, there is no reason you cannot see the results you want to see.

Chapter Takeaways:

- Facebook ads can lead to explosive growth
- Do recon research prior to advertising
- Test different audiences for your ads
- Work on always improving your ad and targeting
- Relevancy score has a big impact on ad performance
- Using questions are great for getting attention

8. THIS COULD SAVE YOUR BUSINESS

Website? Check! Ads? Check! am I done? Nope! This next strategy is one that you should never quit! It was briefly mention in bits and pieces, but it is important to understand just how important split testing is. With your company you will want to constantly try new website looks and ad looks. This is what split testing is. The objective should be to get the best possible result from all parts of your business.

How important is this? Well, it saved my business and it might save yours too! What happened with mine is I initially started advertising and was getting traffic, but no sales. This usually means they are interested in your product, but once they get to your site they are driven away and do not purchase. If you are getting traffic, but no sales this generally means you need to adjust the look or layout of your website. This can be anything from product descriptions, banner images, checkout process, price, or a combination of things.

As we learned early what looks good to you might not look good to the customer. This is why you must test different things! How much should you change at once? When doing split testing with your website, it is very important to only change one thing at once! Remember that! If you begin changing multiple things at once, how will you know what change worked or which one didn't? It will be very difficult to tell and to optimize your site. For example, your website banner might be a picture of a candle and mention your brand name. What if that has been the banner for a while and you have not gotten any sales? Maybe you want to change it to be focused on a sale instead. If you change the banner on your website from "My awesome candle company" to "Two day sale ends tonight!" Perhaps the customer likes that much more and creates an incentive that turns that website traffic into paying customer. While you could change any aspect of your website to make improvements, here are variables you might want to split test first.

- Sales and offers- this might be in the form of bogo sales, percent off sales, limited time sales, fixed dollar amount sales.

- Color scheme-If you have an eco-friendly candle and have a color scheme of red, blue, yellow. Perhaps you could change the color scheme of your website. You might try something like green, brown, and crème.

- Product descriptions- Your product page is the last page they will see be for entering the cart page to proceed to checkout. Having a compelling description that converts is important. You could edit the selling points in the description, add pictures and features or even remove them. It could be that you have to many features and that it looks cluttered.

- Button colors- it is important these stick out and don't blend in too much. You could try to match your desired color scheme or also try something different! Have you ever wondered why so many banks and insurance companies use blue? Blue gives across a message of trust, so maybe if you made your buttons blue the customer will trust your site more!

- Shipping rates- As we mentioned in the shipping section you can change shipping rates that might lead to less abandoned checkouts. This might be a good idea to try everything you can think of for this section because shipping can really scare customers away! It is very important though that you still make sure you are profitable if you are going to discount shipping rates.

- Announcement bar- remember that bar on the top of your website? This is an important part that can really change the customers decision to buy or not. You can try informing the customer of sales, discounted shipping, features, etc. This could change the customers behavior and is something that is definitely worth testing!

- Everything else! – Literally every aspect of your website could be split tested. Any feature or look you have the ability to change could lead to customers liking it more or less. Don't become comfortable with anything on the site unless you are beginning to make consistent sales that are generating you a good profit. If your time could be better spent making candles, make candles, but don't forget you always want to keep improving. That is the key to long term success.

In the advertising portion split testing is as very important. While the role of split testing the website is to turn visitors into customers. The goal of advertising is to turn the most people into website visitors. Split testing can apply for every aspect of advertising and will require creativity. If you are using an influencer they could modify aspects like this:

- Post- How are they displaying your product? What is the comment portion of the post? How are they engaging their audience to drive traffic to your page? Did you give them a custom discount code that they can offer their followers?

- Your profile- when traffic from the influencer visits your company profile how does it look? What are your most recent posts? What is your profile picture? What is your bio?

Even with just using influencers there many different aspects that control the traffic and sales your website will receive. When you notice that an influencer worked better try to compile all the possible differences that lead to a better result and try to fine tune those changes.

   Similar to the ability to change and optimize an influencer the same can be done for Facebook advertising. Change the headline, text, picture, video, etc. There are so many ways to optimize. I need to remind you again you must do this! It is what saved my business and it might save yours too!

SPLIT TESTING JUST FOR ONLINE?:

Absolutely not! Split testing can be used for every aspect of your business, online or not. If you are at an art fair could you split test? Of course! Since art fairs are less often also you could even make a change to your booth ever hour to see what customers react better too. Here are a few things you might optimize at an art fair.

   7.   Physical banner- You could change from focusing on company name and features to a banner that lists all you

promotions/sales.

8. Booth Decorations- These could be quick changes that can end up drawing in more customers to view your booth.

9. Ways to engage customer- For example, perhaps you could have a small bucket of sample candles to hand out to people walking by. If they take one and like it they might turn around and want to buy a bigger candle from you. This is similar to the idea of when you walk around a food court sometimes people will hand out samples of food because if you like it you might end up purchasing more food.

10. Candle layout- just changing the layout of your candles make more people want to stop and smell them? Does it make it easier for the customer to browse you selection?

CONCLUSION:

Do not forget the rule to split test! No matter your method of selling, always think about what ways you could split test. If you have newsletter subscribers on your site or people visiting your booth, it might be even worth it to offer a free candle in exchange for advice on what you could do to make your booth better. The key to this is honest advice. No one wants to hurt someone's feelings, let them know that critical suggestions will ultimately help your business thrive and that even critiques are appreciated.

Chapter Takeaways:
- If you can change something, it can be split tested
- Split testing sales and promotions can see very effective
- Split testing can apply to influencers
- Split testing at art fairs could be on a schedule of every 30-60 minutes
- Ask for constructive feedback
- Do not avoid split testing, it is **VERY** important

9. THE #1 KEY TO SUCCESS

I appreciate the dedication and hard work you have put in to read this book. Education is the best way to improve your chances succeeding in the candle business and you should be proud of taking action to take the necessary steps to make that dream a reality. I hope that I was able to offer an immense amount of value in this book. I hope you will be able to take this information and create your own wildly successful candle business!

It is import to reflect on all the steps you learned in this book. Every step usually depends on another step to be completed. You couldn't begin advertising if you didn't design a candle. You probably wouldn't have a candle designed unless you picked a niche that you were going to target. You couldn't advertise unless a website had been designed.

You see every aspect of the business creation relies on another factor to be completed. When you complete each segment of the creation process you move closer to being able to turn your hobby into a profitable business! It should be exciting and fun!

If you run into trouble completing these steps or you question if your candle product is the right idea, remember you can always pivot! If you picked a niche you don't like do not be afraid to make changes. It doesn't mean you failed, it was a bad idea, or any of that! It is a learning experience and just like learning from a book, it will make you a better candle maker and a better candle business owner.

WHERE TO START?:

Do you know what I have seen kill the most candles businesses? Here is what is not the number one killer of most candle business ideas:

- It is not bad advertising
- A bad website
- A bad product

- A poor sales pitch
- The wrong niche
- No money
- No time
- The wrong color scheme
- The wrong label
- The wrong wax

The number one killer of most business ideas does not even come close to any of those potential issues. So what is it? LACK OF EXECUTION! Do not fall victim to a lack of execution. Since you made it this far, I believe you will have the will power to begin executing. Starting a new business can be a very intimidating thing. If you are afraid to execute, that can waste your time and rip all of that potential right from you.

What do I recommend? Begin to execute! This could be anything here are a couple quick ways you can begin to execute and smash that fear of starting:

- Draw a candle design
- Create a logo
- Pick a company name
- Create a company Facebook page
- Tell your friends and family- I have found this to actually be super helpful! They will ask you how your project is coming which will add a little bit of obligation so you are able to tell them about your progress.
- Buy website domain name
- Make a candle
- Pick a niche and write down every

possible feature your candle could have

It is just important to start taking action. What happens often is that I see the people get the idea and all of the sudden tasks get put off and never end up completed. The best way to avoid that is just by making the first step. Even if it is as simple as just coming up with your company name.

WHY YOU MUST EXECUTE:

This comes down to somewhat being opinion based but I believe you must execute this candle business because of one reason. Regret, my biggest fear when I thought about it was getting to an older age and regretting the things I wanted to do, but never had the courage to do. To me, I wanted to do things on my own terms, you may feel a different way or have a different drive. That is ok! However, you cannot forget you picked up this book to educate yourself and how to start a business of your own doing what you love. To me, it seems that would be much easier to forgive yourself if you tried your best, but failed. Compared to never giving it your best shot and not knowing what could have happened. I feel fortunate to have not only built a successful candle business, but to now have the time and experience to write this book and help everyone else that has that same dream. Whether you are trying to make a side hustle income or replace your full time, it starts with execution.

Put this book down and start executing!

ABOUT THE AUTHOR

Who is Matthew Heintschel? Matthew is an expert in the candle industry and is known for creating one of the fastest growing candle companies in the country. In just a few months he took a business that had $0 in sales to generating over $200,000 a month in sales! After selling his candle business, he has turned and dedicated his time to helping others achieve their dream in the candle industry.

65851305R00064

Made in the USA
Middletown, DE
06 September 2019